Love, Attention, and Affection

Love, Attention, and Affection

JAMES R. DIXON

LOVE, ATTENTION, AND AFFECTION

iUniverse books may be ordered through booksellers or by contacting:

iUniverse
1663 Liberty Drive
Bloomington, IN 47403
www.iuniverse.com
1-800-Authors (1-800-288-4677)

Because of the dynamic nature of the Internet, any web addresses or links contained in this book may have changed since publication and may no longer be valid. The views expressed in this work are solely those of the author and do not necessarily reflect the views of the publisher, and the publisher hereby disclaims any responsibility for them.

Any people depicted in stock imagery provided by Thinkstock are models,
and such images are being used for illustrative purposes only.
Certain stock imagery © Thinkstock.

ISBN: 978-1-4917-8155-5 (sc)
ISBN: 978-1-4917-8156-2 (e)

Library of Congress Control Number: 2015918350

Print information available on the last page.

iUniverse rev. date: 11/19/2015

Foreword

Love, Attention, and Affection is a three-part story elaborating on my trials and tribulations in relationships. As I wade through the murky waters of relationships, I've received each of the three components intermittently, but never together. Love is what I want. Attention is what I need. However, affection is what I receive. With this book I aspire to ignite healthy conversations with people as to what components are necessary in order to obtain and maintain a successful relationship.

Love, Attention, and Affection is comprised of three individual stories. But, collectively the three stories combine to tell one ultimate story. Each individual story is represented by a particular color that generalizes the emotions and sentiments of the story. Love is represented by red. Attention correlates to yellow. Affection is strongly associated with purple. There is a wide array of poetic styles that are used to tell various stories. The poetic styles that are used include, but are not limited to diamante, cinquain, quinzaine, ode, and free verse. What makes this book relatable to readers are the various plot twists that create an emotional rollercoaster-like feeling.

Love

Love/Red

Love can be strongly associated with the color red. Fire and blood are ignited by the color red.

Red is affiliated with spontaneity, fortitude, vulnerability, aggression, and sovereignty. Red can also represent infatuation, desire, and love.

Red is a fierce color. It represents warning and danger as it provides the human mind the ability to make sudden decisions. It raises blood pressure due to its high visibility, rich density, and thin texture. In the same way, it resembles the infatuation, desire, and love humankind may have for someone, or something through emotions.

Red is one of various colors resembling the color of love. It is the most versatile color in the color spectrum. For this reason, it is the most popular color used on the internet to portray sales and clearance signs. Red is used a lot in advertising as well. It is the one common color embedded on the flags of many countries in the world to display strength, courage, and honor. Finally, red is the color most commonly used by mankind to elicit amorous feelings (red lips, lady in red, red-light districts, etc).

Other color variations of red include: light red, pink, dark red, brown, and reddish-brown.

Light red represents enthusiasm, sensuality, infatuation, sympathy, and affection.

Pink signifies courtship, fondness, and friendship. It denotes feminine qualities and disinterest.

Dark red is associated with vitality, firmness, resentment, fury, authority, audacity, bitterness, and acrimony.

Brown suggests cohesion and denotes masculine qualities.

Reddish-brown is correlated with harvest and fall.

Love

Angel In My Dreams

Phenomenal woman who commands my undivided attention

You're a witness to your personality serving as the center of my weakness

Your essence has me spinning in a whole other direction

I never opened up to you because I felt I'd be disrespecting

When I look into my kaleidoscope I see your reflection

Expecting you to show me your true feelings

Maybe that was just me wishfully thinking

Or was I thinking wishfully while suffering in my own misery

I received the news about you having your second baby

While that's beautiful for you, that's bad news for me

Besides you having your first child, then getting married

That's the third sign a relationship with us will never be

James R. Dixon

Brokenhearted I felt; so I had to make you a distant memory

While dying from a broken heart, hearing from you became my remedy

Mission accomplished, but I still haven't officially let you go

Nor will I ever; so I'll continue to hold that small strand of hope

Call it whipped, sprung, or whatever you want

I'm done hiding my feelings; I was dying to give you what you wanted

At the lowest point in my life you were with me

To let me know love is in sight and for that I wanted you near me

Your husband might develop bad feelings, or see me as a threat

This shows how much I don't care otherwise I would've kept it a secret

But, simultaneously I need you to read this as the message is true

The angel in my dreams was brought to life in the form of you

With it being too late now, I have to live with the thought of not having you

Tossing and turning in my sleep; you can't imagine how this is affecting me

Some nights I find myself questioning if the angel in my dreams was real

The answers came to mind as I thought of your sex appeal

I guess the angel in my dreams was just a fantasy; what a tragedy

Just when I was ready to wipe and dine you your majesty

Another dream turned into reality; I felt it had to be

Hopefully we can remain friends; I would never want you mad at me

You asked of me to always wish you the best; I answered "yes" gladly

I felt my heart deteriorating in my chest when you walked away sadly

I had no worries because I knew you would be okay

Because of you, I pray for a strong woman to enter my life every day

What I Can't Have

Why is it that

I always want what I can't have

I wanted to give you

Everything he gave you and more

Literally!

Imagine me rushing home

From a low paying, dead end night job

To take care of you

Doing the things your husband

And father of your children

Wouldn't dare do

Massage your scalp, rub your feet

Cook and clean

Learn Spanish as a second language

To communicate with you

More effectively

I would've traded it all

For an opportunity

To stand across from you

At the altar

To proclaim you my wife

To start our own life

To impregnate you twice

Share kisses with you

Until my feelings suffice

How far be it for me to

Lust over a former friend's wife

Stabbing him in the back

Though he didn't give me the knife

Needless to say, her love wasn't up for grabs

Why is it that

I always want what I can't have

James R. Dixon

Senryu Intermission

I once stooped to an all time low
to find love.
Was I that desperate?

True love can be hard to find. That is if you search for it. However, I felt it can come to me in the most mysterious ways. One way was pursuing an old friend's wife. Pursuing her was negligence on my behalf. Or was it? Seeing as to how she once showed a similar interest in me.

The One

When will I find the one?

The one who excites my five senses

The one who is humble and pretentious

The one who utilizes her strengths to help the weak

The one who optimizes the essence of me

When will I find the one?

The one who I'm infatuated with

The one who I'm relentless in making love with

The one whose love for me can fill an ocean

The one whose passionate feelings for me are open

When will I find the one?

The one who helps me to be a better man

The one who is courageous and understands

The one she has in front of her and isn't too blind to see

The one she has loves her as much as she loves me

When will I find the one?

The one who isn't afraid to give me her heart

The one I can build a bond with that no one can tear apart

The one who my family cares about

The one who I love and can't live without

When will I find the one?

First Date

Meeting her online
as opposed to in person
was perfect.
Until she asked me
the most dreadful question;

When can we have our first date?

Every passing day
her patience wore thin.
Her anxiety to meet me grew thick
leaving her to
abandon the criteria
of chivalry and
ask me on a date that coming weekend.

Needless to say
I was nervous.

My first impressions
tend to be full of
awkward adrenalin.
So I thought I'd
download a dating application,
or better yet
order a dating book
thinking $6.99
plus shipping and handling
would teach me how to be
a perfect gentleman.

Date night was accompanied
by subtle hesitation.

I compared personality traits
to that of her online profile
while she dominated
the conversation.

My mind was
preoccupied by her every word
while my stomach was
consuming steak, salmon, and potatoes.
Her diagnosis of her
characteristics served as the
finest things I've ever heard.

The top of the night
was mellow.
Reiterating our previous
conversations with the addition
of flirtatious comments
capped off with a kiss
that made my legs fragile.

Cinquain
First dates
beyond stressful
you prepare for the worst
often times they produce the best
results

Conversations

Day one after our first date
Produced nerves and anxiety
No text message, no phone call
No e-mail, no response at all
No conversations since that date
Time is of the essence

Desperation sets in
I began having doubts
Cyber stalking was in full effect
I stalked all of her social media accounts
Her Instagram, her Flickr
Her Facebook, her Twitter
Her MySpace to see her thoughts
I even stalked her Tumblr and her BlogSpot

Nothing would appease my desperation
Accept remanences of conversations
Reassuring me her feelings are mutual
I'm intrigued; hopefully she feels the same way
Despite my sweaty palms, slurred words
Silence and awkwardness on the first date

Cinquain
Convos
can go two ways
good, bad; happy, or sad
they draw two people close when they
converse

Senryu Intermission

Good education, great career.
Something's missing,
or maybe someone!

First dates are excruciatingly difficult to prepare for. I don't know which is more burdensome: preparing for a first date, or the mental warfare that plagues my mind upon completion of the date. Did I make a good first impression? Did she enjoy the date? Did I say too much? Did I not say enough? These questions and many more plague my mind throughout the remainder of the night.

Someday

I want to be loved someday

To the point that I would alter my appearance

I would purchase a new wardrobe the day after a clearance

Desecrate my body and become more adherent

I want to be loved someday

To the point that I would alter my personality

Sacrifice my morals and adopt your mentality

Dialogue with logic remnant of your rationality

I want to be loved someday

To the point that I would alter my nutrition

I would eat what appeases you to garner your attention

Drink inebriant concoctions you enjoy every tradition

I want to be loved someday

To the point that I would alter my physique

Incorporate a diet and fitness technique

Strengthen my arms, tighten my abs, and my oblique

I want to be loved someday

To the point that I would alter my priorities

Create a union similar to that of sororities

I deem you principle owner of my authorities

I want to be loved someday

To the point that I would alter my life

I would give anything to find a lover and friend in a wife

In hopes to be loved someday

Second Date

The kickoff was consistent.
To say we picked up
where we left off
is an understatement.

Apparently

Absence makes the
heart grow fonder.
The bashful look on her face
displayed her excitement
at seeing me. Her two
public displays of affection
helped to ease
the awkward tension.

Traditionally

The man pays for every date.
But it was nice to see
her take a non-chauvinistic approach
and treat me to something we both can relate.

Intense conversation was essential.
Reiterating intimate conversations
previously generalized in message text.

What's your career path as a civilian?
Does your future include marriage and children?
How are you perceived by your ex?
Do you believe in premarital sex?
Have you encountered any STD's?
Do your sex partners exceed three?

All answers were prevalent.
Igniting a flame so big
all other priorities became irrelevant.

Quinzaine
Confusion weighs on my mind
Does she not like me?
Or does she?

James R. Dixon

Senryu Intermission

Excitement comes over me
when meeting one
with common interests.

Relationships tend to be an outer body experience. You work hard to obtain it. Then you work even harder to maintain it. As for myself, I often times lose myself in the process. I try to convince myself that it is love I'm fighting for. As the cliché goes "love will make a person do some crazy things."

What Is Love

What is love?

Love is the idea that two could exist in harmony

One ignites emotions the other can be shy to speak

Finding commonalities with a vigorous technique

Admiring one's naturalness, graceful soul, and physique

Love is care!

What is love?

Love is the evolution of feelings one slightly doubts

Making your knees fragile around the one you care about

The person's heart you travel to taking various routes

The affection you have for the one you can't live without

Love is infatuation!

James R. Dixon

What is love?

Love is making your partner not feel lone and secluded

Sharing your life to prevent them from being excluded

Not being combative when you think one's points aren't lucid

Supporting your partner's hobbies though you find them stupid

Love is patience!

What is love?

Love is making someone feel good; fervidly protected

Making one feel mentally and physically respected

Stimulating your partner in ways they feel affected

Holding them in your arms so they never feel neglected

Love is security!

What is love?

Love is building trust and honesty through conversation

Putting your wants aside to build a better foundation

Standing by your partner through troublesome situations

Fighting through tough times rather than thinking separation

Love is sacrifice!

Quinzaine
I think I love my girlfriend
Do we both know love?
What is love?

Those Three Words

**I've always anticipated me telling you
Those Three Words**

That could alter our relationship
That could define love in increments
Through love, attention, and affection
The affinity of two sexes

Bounded by a mutual consent
Both our minds, bodies, and souls convinced
We're in sync with no speculation
The affinity of two sexes

**I've always anticipated you telling me
Those Three Words**

That's inscribed on the heart in your chest
That's spelled in blood that you bleed to death
Through your mind ignites the thought process
The affinity of two sexes

Bounded by a conjoint parliament
Both our love, fervor, and hearts evinced
We're in sync with no contemplation
The affinity of two sexes

Honeymoon Phase

Conversations often
got muddled.
Glimpses of previous relationships
ceased to exist
due to our unification
being subtle.

Her hugs would relieve my stress.
My chest pressed against her breasts
while inhaling the scent of her
perfume arising from her neck.

Her slight kisses upon my cheek
made my hands grip
tighter around her physique.
My body was tensing up
from physical arousal
as she slowly undressed me.

Her orgasmic sigh of relief
as I penetrated gave me
a sense of responsibility.

I felt I had to stimulate her
mentally, physically, and emotionally.

I was so engulfed in sexual activity
I disregarded the fact that
she owed the same fiduciary duty to me.

James R. Dixon

Could this be what expressing
love in the highest form
of gratitude feels like?

Hummingbirds singing in trees,
fireworks exploding, and
the climactic altitude of ejaculation
sending numbness through my body!

My tense body starts feeling weak.
Upon the finish, the two of us each
gaze into each other's eyes as if
we will be together for eternity.

Cinquain
Romance
creates a bond
where we can heighten our
love, attention, and affection
through sex

Senryu Intermission

I fantasize:
dimmed lights,
scented candles,
ocean views,
me holding you.

In the genesis of a new relationship, I have a habit of trying to orchestrate the entire relationship as opposed to letting things develop organically. That is until we experience sexual intercourse for the first time. Many feel that sexual intercourse is just a physical act between two people. It's an accentuated feeling for me. It's the emotions that tie into it that alters my mental stability.

Enchanted Love

I speak about you my enchanted love!

My heart caught just a glimpse of what could be
A detailed monument of you and me
Selflessness; there's no "I" with you, it's "we"
My heart caught just a glimpse of what could be

My heart reveals thoughts I was blind to see
My fantasy could be reality
Delighted I am; thinking unity
My heart reveals thoughts I was blind to see

I think about you my enchanted love!

My heart sought visions of you in white light
Elegance and beauty captured my sights
Allured and enthralled; what seemed wrong felt right
My heart sought visions of you in white light

My heart screams words my mouth is shy to speak
Through rain, hail, sleet, and snow, it's you I seek
Love, attention, affection; my heart's weak
My heart screams words my mouth is shy to speak

I dream about you my enchanted love!

My heart's soaring at the thought of your touch
Striving to conjure words that mean so much
Love, sex, passion; I confess dreams of such
My heart's soaring at the thought of your touch

My heart's soaring from my dreams of your love
Fierce kisses followed by passionate hugs
Soul's entwining; heart's pounding from what was
My heart's soaring from my dreams of your love

<u>Quinzaine</u>
I dream of enchanted love
Why do I dream big?
Do you dream?

When She's With Me

When she's not with me, life is utterly brutal

When she's not with me, I am dull and frugal

When she's not with me, my rationale is wretched

When she's not with me, I feel lonesome and desperate

When she's not with me, life is absolutely miserable

But, when she's with me, life is beautiful

When she's with me, life is entirely refined

When she's with me, I am effective; yet confined

When she's with me, my intuition is ceremonial

When she's with me, I feel befriended and jovial

When she's with me, life is precisely exhilarating

Senryu Intermission

When she's not with me
life is tragic!
When she's with me
I'm ecstatic!

When in love, I get so engulfed in the relationship to the point nothing else matters. I neglect everything and everyone around me. My clingy habits become exposed as I express my feelings through sonnets, nonets, quatrains, and quinzaines.

The First Time

Every time we *talk*, it feels like the first time!

      Daily multi-hour conversations that stimulate my mind
      Your tranquilizing voice makes my body unwind; after a long day
      I'd masturbate to thoughts of you the whole time
      Orchestrating our relationship before your interest declines

Every time we *hug*, it feels like the first time!

      Your arms wrapped around my neck; mine wrapped around your thighs
      Your right hand grazing my left cheek as you lustfully look into my eyes
      Emotionally unstable; at times I would break down and cry
      From us holding each other while we express how we feel inside

Every time we *kiss*, it feels like the first time!

      You placing my right hand on your left breast to get me aroused
      A California king bed outlined with roses and candles for you to be bowsed
      Sexual chemistry igniting a fire too big to be dowsed
      Generating impromptu thoughts as to getting you espoused

Every time we *make love*, it feels like the first time!

      Sparking intense, intimate conversations brimming with sarcasm
      Kissing you from your neck to your breasts prompting romantic phantasms
      Performing oral sex on you until you have a clitoral orgasm
      Penetrating your vagina via numerous positions causing back spasms

The Peak

The peak is the point in the hierarchy you never think you would reach
    The sickly feeling in your stomach when you feel intrigued
        The peak is when love, attention, and affection are in sync
            The peak is the moment you realize that love is no longer extinct

The peak is the unspoken bond that two people share
    The reminiscing of past times while awaiting the future you two prepared
        The peak is supporting one another through sadness and despair
            The peak is celebrating the good times with a companion who cares

The peak is elevating your relationship to the highest cliff with no fear of falling
    The ability to confide in someone who's practical in problem solving
        The peak is relegating your pride and ego to avoid verbal brawling
            The peak is the unification of two people with no name calling

The peak is standing across from your loved one at the alter
    The pledging of biblical allegiance; pronouncing commands so you don't falter
        The peak is making love to the idea of being a mother and a father
            The peak is multiplying your family via reproduction of a son and/or daughter

James R. Dixon

Senryu Intermission

First Date, The First Time,
and The Peak ignites
our romantic chemistry.

When in love, you feel like it could never end. For many people, myself included, the future entails marriage and children. Although seemingly far away, the future can feel much closer when in love.

What Happened

We were in route to reaching the peak
However, several detours immobilized our mental harmony
Attempts at reconciliation were rescinded by her
Tyrannical responses as she refused to conform

However, that was the calm before the storm
Arguments would lead for hours
Pots and plates angrily slammed on the kitchen counter
Perhaps this could be the
End of our relationship which I fear
Neighbors calling the cops because they began to hear
Estranged noises which was just us having sex before her
Departure the next morning

Attention

Attention/Yellow

Attention can be strongly associated with the color yellow. Yellow is the color of sunshine. It is affiliated with indulgence, jubilation, acumen, and energy.

Yellow produces a warning effect. It is commonly used to arouse awareness of caution. It is the color that represents decay, sickness, and jealousy. On the contrary, yellow stimulates the mental capabilities of mankind. In the same way, it generates muscle energy. Yellow is an attention grabbing color that ignites one's vulnerable feelings towards another.

Yellow is a sympathetic color used to evoke pleasurable, refreshing emotions. It is the primary color between green and orange in the color spectrum. Yellow is the least versatile color in the color spectrum. Men perceive yellow to be a lighthearted, childish color. However, women perceive yellow as an attention getter. The few multiple shades of yellow provoke different meanings. Lighter shades of yellow insinuate the desire of one to elucidate his/her feelings towards another person. Highlights of yellow are most popularly used in romantic cards spouses give to each other.

Yellow can cause a disturbing effect on people if frequently used to represent various entities.

It is well documented that infants tend to cry more in yellow rooms. When placed against black, yellow stands out more creating a warning due to the combination of the two colors. Yellow indicates attention, prestige, and allegiance. Furthermore, yellow has also been connected to cowardice behavior.

Other color variations of yellow include: dull (dingy) yellow and light yellow.

Dull (dingy) yellow represents caution, deterioration, illness, and jealousy.

Light yellow is associated with intellect, inventiveness, and comfort.

Attention

Where Did You Go
Exotic Temptress
Emancipated Emotions
Breakdowns In Communication
I've Longed
Rejection
The Morning After
Better Than The Rest
She Said I'm Too Much
The Break Up I
Died In Your Arms
He Lay
Psychedelic Relic
Last Poem For You
Epitaph On My Heart

Where Did You Go

I fell asleep one night and had a weird dream
That took place in an early morning of spring

It was a rude awakening as I rolled over to touch your arm
I woke up early that morning to realize you were gone

I could only think of what happened the night before
I tried to settle the score, but you weren't happy anymore

I understand our fight was brutal, but you leaving wasn't the answer
It tore me up inside not knowing your whereabouts

Here I am feeling stupid thinking you would come back
On the couch I sat and sat playing old Boys 2 Men tracks

On the verge of having an anxiety attack
Leaving countless messages on your phone and no call back

So I send you this as my apology in the rainy weather
It tears me up inside; I can't keep my emotions together

So I'm writing you this detailed letter today
I want to reconcile and hopefully you feel the same way

I woke up in the middle of that night nervous
Thanking God it was only a dream as I gave her a kiss

As I explained to her what happened; she laughed and said this
"Our relationship is filled with bliss so don't stress"

James R. Dixon

Senryu Intermission

Broke and decrepit I felt
at the thought of you
leaving me for good.

What benefits are there to obtaining everything you dream of if it means losing yourself in the process? That is a question I ask myself every time I get involved in a relationship. Evidently, I put my relationship partners before my personal and career goals. Till this day, I struggle to find a balance.

Exotic Temptress

I'm debating if it's personality or physical attraction
Because you're so attractive
Either way I have been noticing your beauty back then
Even till this day nothing's changed
I felt I've connected all the pieces to the puzzle
Then you changed the game
Years have gone by and I still don't have you
Who am I to blame?
Myself! Although the tunnels of love were written in your name
So please explain;
Why my mind gets stuck in a trance when I hear your name
This repeated cycle of emotions gets me mentally deranged
Insidious habits multiplied within an instant
As you questioned my interest
I explained the difference
In celebratory fashion in hopes you would become more existent
My exotic temptress; as mentioned
Tension is building from not having you
Please come release it
Come make my life magnificent; as of now, it's decent

Emancipated Emotions

I approached you through the emotions of my emancipation
Translation,
I bared my soul in hopes for a token of your appreciation
In other words,
My frustration has been raging from not being able to hug and touch your loving nation
Needless to say,
Masturbation endured its multiplication from lacking patience
On the other hand,
My miseducation about you coerces contemplation on seeking admiration
For this reason,
I have an infatuation for sending you salutations regarding us having relations
With this in mind,
My gyration is stationed around your heavenly destination
In the meantime,
My continuation to gain your heart elates my motivation
To sum it all up,
There are several stages to your evaluation with no exaggeration
In conclusion,
I approached you through the emotions of my emancipation

Cinquain
Poems
written to show
how I feel about her
emancipated emotions
are real

Breakdowns In Communication

Anxiety builds prior to our next encounter.

I would go days and weeks without seeing her.

Her lack of love and attention

created a lot of awkward tension.

I couldn't pay her to give an affectionate greeting.

A one armed hug and a kiss on the cheek.

All I could think was

Grandma's apple pie gave me a bigger erection.

She verbalized 50/50 love

though to my nescience, she pre-wrote her retraction.

Mind games were intense.

Communication was irrelevant.

She would give me the wink, double eyelid bat,

plush grin, with a slight head nod,

then watch me fall into the same trap all over again.

Feeling like I always lose and can't win!

Perhaps I was in love with the idea of being in love.

Maybe the impassioned hugs,

the slight kisses on the cheek,

and my hands transitioning

from emphatically caressing her breasts

to a tight grip around her posterior

was the perfect antidote for my addiction.

What else did I possibly expect?

Lackluster affection tends to

make me forget about my

morals, integrity, and self respect.

Senryu Intermission

One day I'm writing
you love poems.
The next, I'm appalled
by your actions.

The highs were the highs and the lows were the lows. As previously stated, the peak is "elevating your relationship to the highest cliff with no fear of falling." I find it hard to believe we can go from being immensely in love with each other one day to verbally abusing each other the next.

I've Longed

One month

Two weeks

Three days

Four hours

Five minutes

Six seconds

That was how long it took for me to realize I loved you
I've longed to find the perfect way to express my feeling
Cards and candy wouldn't suffice my emotional breakthrough
Flowers and jewelry are delightful, but still not too appealing

A home cooked candlelit dinner wasn't good enough for you
Maybe a scavenger hunt leading to me reciting poetry about my feeling
An intimate night while stargazing may ignite my emotional breakthrough
Or writing them in the snow lined with candles would be more appealing

Quinzaine
I have strong feelings for you
Do you feel the same?
Do we match?

Rejection

At times it hurt to look at you
Painful thoughts tend to resurface|
Your smile and grace inflaming your beauty
I coward with the feeling of attempting
To speak this dream into existence
My contained feelings and emotions
Causes me to act strange
I'm a deranged person's spokes model
Trying to discover the proper words
At the bottom of a vodka bottle

I'm Nervous

Touching your hand will cause my energy to go insane
Like combining hydrogen and nitrogen
To a cell membrane
If I get inconceivable thoughts when I look at you
Just imagine what a kiss will do
Liable to send me into a hypochondria like coma
Just at the thought of that visual
In my mind, my feelings are tangible
Though to you they're invisible

James R. Dixon

Senryu Intermission

You reject my advances,
then accuse me of not
trying that hard.

Often times I feel like I'm the king of coming up short. My apologies continue to fall on deaf ears. Desperately, I write her more letters, poems, and songs. She then tells me "I will love you however you need me to love you." For some reason, I can't find a way to tell her she's wrong.

The Morning After

Good girls typically like bad guys!

But at what point does a good girl demand a good guy
Maybe you're unclear of the perks, rewards, and benefits
I'm a good guy, but through your pain, you will never see
    the difference

I'll treat you like a queen; as I explain what this means
I know what you're thinking; I've heard this all before
But these words aren't coming from the mouth of a lying,
    deceitful boy

They're coming from a phenomenal man who thinks the world of you
A man who looks in the mirror, then sees your face, and says "this is
    the one for you"

I like you, but my like will soon turn to love!

With more touches of your hands followed by more hugs
These aren't my final words, but just my current thoughts
After waking up in your bed, the scent of your perfume is what
    I caught

I laid in your sheets allowing them to caress my body
All I could think of was all the joy to me you've brought

Cinquain
Today
I reflect on
all the mistakes I've made
that put us in the place we were
last night

51

Better Than The Rest

Sex is the unification between woman and man

Not between boy and girl who's too young to understand

What it's like not to disband; please understand

You don't have to feed the sexual appetite of an abusive man

You are beautiful! You need to understand you need a man

Who deems the two of you in sync just by the touch of your hands

I understand how difficult it is to practice abstinence

But keep in mind you don't need a man to define your happiness

A positive example was contingent upon your father's absence

But pregnancy and diseases are the results of your careless actions

Your body is a temple! If you mistreat it what happens?

Men have sex with you, leave you, and then refer to you in past tense

Take a moment to look at your life and realize you've been blessed

With gifts to share to prevent from being promiscuous

Every day you wake up, life is a test

Just keep in mind you are better than the rest

She Said I'm Too Much

She said I'm too much

I'm too much because I don't address her as if she is a whore to me

I'm too much because I make her a top priority

I'm too much because I care

I'm too much because I question her when other men stop and stare

She said I'm too much

I'm too much because I sympathize with her when she cries

I'm too much because I console her by wiping tears from her eyes

I'm too much because I'm attentive and I write her poetry

I'm too much because I spare no expense to get her to notice me

She said I'm too much

I'm too much because I have three college degrees and a lifestyle she can't dictate

I'm too much because I have a small business and a career with a 401(k)

I'm too much because my relationship rectitude doesn't make her irate

I'm too much because I'm not a loser like all the other men she used to date

James R. Dixon

She said I'm too much

I'm too much because I'm her spiritual brother, lover, and friend

I'm too much because I proclaimed I'll love her till the bitter end

I'm too much because I articulate my thoughts in ways she doesn't understand

I'm too much because I contemplated titling this poem "Contradictions Heedless

Women Place On A Good Man"

She said I'm too much

I'm too much because I want more

I'm too much because I don't define chivalry as "fulfilling a chore"

I'm too much because I want stability

I'm too much because I won't settle for anything less than trustworthiness,

honesty, peace, and tranquility

<u>Quinzaine</u>
How dare she say I'm too much
Is she not enough?
Well, is she?

Senryu Intermission

Trying to appease
hormonal women
whose futile
was a mistake.

First women claim they want a gentleman. They say they want a man who to a degree still believes in chivalry. Naturally, I give them that! They then say I'm too nice and I should consider being more aggressive. Me being naïve and desperate to prove I'm not futile; I began to adopt juvenile characteristics. Upon completion of my transformation, they then say I'm a jerk and I should just be myself. Needless to say, compromising my morals and integrity for a thick waist, DD breasts, and a gorgeous smile got me nowhere.

The Break Up

Internally we calculate the space

between the earth and the sun

> That distance in kilometers
>
> is the space you put between us

Motivated to capture your heart;

I felt I'd be winning

> I wasn't spiritually led in the present;
>
> I was emotionally driven by the fairytale ending

Where do I begin to make up the time she took

> She stole my soul and livelihood like a thief in the night
>
> > There's no trace of her for miles; trust me, I've looked

I DON'T UNDERSTAND!

I feel completely abandoned, lonely, and desolate

> All I'm left with is an empty one bedroom apartment
>
> > With thoughts as to why our relationship couldn't be salvaged

Ferocious arguments would lead to a cold make-up

> Making it effortless to design and compose the break up

Died In Your Arms

Love...

Heartbreak...

Depression...

The three seemed adjacent!

Every night my body goes to bed
But unstable thoughts run through my head
I struggle to put them to rest
I constantly think about the love we once had
My love for you spoke loud and clear
Even though you questioned my devotion
I replayed multiple conversations
Lingering on every word
To capture your every emotion
To write a poem so potent
Opening the windows of my soul
So you could envision the mind state
I was in when I wrote it

Notice: the substantial amount of feelings I pour

My heart is outspoken

Notice: the ten tears I've shed on your shoulder

Helped me to savor this moment

He Lay

He Lay: Helpless

Fidgeting in his sleep

He sits upright in a corner

Awaken by relentless shaking and crying

Questioning God saying "why is this happening to me"

He Lay: Motionless

Resisting his emotional demons

Prohibiting him from rising to his feet

Seeking justification through humankind treatment

He asks for the support of his ex-girlfriend while grieving

<u>Cinquain</u>
He lay
empty, distraught
damaged beyond repair
defenseless; motionless he lay
broken

Senryu Intermission

I felt it's detrimental
to my health
not having you in my life.

As I begin to mourn the loss of a girlfriend, she shows no remorse in her decision to let me go. She spoke as if she felt justified in her actions while simultaneously discrediting everything I've done for her.

Psychedelic Relic

My first months of life with you I thought were the best
Equated into a relationship I thought was a test
The first half was pure bliss; I then felt blessed
As for other women, I trusted you and forsook the rest
It wasn't the sex or support you gave me
It wasn't the way you dressed or way you saved me
It was the emotional stress that seemed to elate me
For some reason I was attracted to crazy ladies

Through the he say she say, all you knew were lies about me
If you never loved me, why would you cry about me
I lived after you saying "you will die without me"
I survived after you claiming "there's no life without me"

It's no longer unbeknownst as to why I loved you
I thought I put that life in back of me
I don't understand why this continues to happen to me
Although I fall in love easy, I fall out very quickly

As I live and breathe, it's hard to think and see
My vision was impaired by what seemed to be
Reality unfortunately mistaken for just a dream
Killing me softly; causing me to star in my own autobiography
You architected my demise sponsoring the rise and fall of me
Ceilings crashing, walls closing, circle is smaller, and I'm feeling lonely
Bringing me back to God, the only one who could console me
It's no longer you, now I look for his word to console me

We were on the same page physically, but not mentally
Which ranks low of importance; you weren't meant for me
Being with you, my behavior was disgusting and full of grief
The fact that you approved of it put me in disbelief

I questioned if you were in love with my benevolence, or me
I vowed not to settle for less again; you didn't deserve me
You slandered me, berated me, and tried to derail my dreams
Through all of that I still loved you though you intentionally hurt me

Last Poem For You

Where do I begin

    To tell you how I feel

        Never thought I'd be

            Making this transition

So soon it's surreal

    I feel my heart sinking

        Love and trust is gone

            All's left is how I feel

Emotionally incapacitated

I felt losing you would be my biggest fear

The number of tears I shed

Totals the number of words that fell on deaf ears

A heart once shaped pure

    Is now disproportioned

        It's sore, scared, and bruised

            Severely vandalized

The blemishes grew

    My mind state is frantic

        Feelings are suppressed

            In this last poem for you

Mentally unstable

Mood swings causing unpredictable actions

I find myself doing

Irrational things to get your slightest reaction

James R. Dixon

Senryu Intermission

The end was near!
I thought compromising my morals would make
her stay.

After analyzing my shortcomings, I feel like a tainted wishing well. Despite all of my deposits, I still continue to fail. I say failure is not an option, but this time I may have to accept it. It's like trying to find a job in a recession; opportunities are limited.

Epitaph On My Heart

Land of sorrow

Ocean of tears

Valley of death

End of life

LOVE briefly summarizes the epitaph on my heart

The two years of tears I cried in three days glow in the dark

Senryus, sonnets, and monodies administered my start

To disclose the numerous reasons why we're apart

Quinzaine
The epitaph on my heart
What's the inscription?
Will she cry?

Affection

Affection/Purple

Affection can be associated with the color purple. Purple is the combination of the security of blue and the energy of red. In addition to purple being associated with affection, it is also associated with royalty. It is the prime color that symbolizes power, grandeur, opulence, and aspiration. As a matter of fact, it evokes prosperity and luxury. Other personality traits and/or characteristics that purple represents include: poise, decency, self-sufficiency, creativity, subtlety, and fascination.

According to research I've conducted, seventy percent of children in their pre-adolescent years of life embrace purple more than any other color in the color spectrum. This is in large parts due to its scarcity in nature. Many people feel that it is so rare to the point that it could be artificial.

As it pertains to the marketplace, light purple, or lavender is considered a good choice for a feminine design. Bright purple would be best utilized when promoting children's products.

Other color variations of purple include: light purple and dark purple.

Light purple evokes romantic and nostalgic feelings.

Dark purple evokes anguish and somber feelings.

Affection

The Break Up II
Love Turned To Lust
Somehow
Incompatible
Behind Wounded Eyes
My Picture, Your Picture
Ode To Nice Guys
Everything
Disclaimer
The Clean Up Man
Slip Away I
Slip Away II
Slip Away III
Relationship Revelation
Dear Future Wife

The Break Up II

In three days I've cried two years worth of tears

All the "I love yous" and "I miss yous" fell on deaf ears

Intimidated to leave her due to her spiteful sheer posts

While brainwashed from reliving the seductive words I hear most

"I can see passion in your eyes; your dimples enlighten your smile"

Plush grin on my face from words I haven't heard in a while

Replaying countless conversations we had one year in autumn

Only to realize sex was the only thing we had in common

James R. Dixon

Countless questions unanswered; now I only question how to move on

My commencement forms by rewriting old letters, poems, and songs

That was originally written to capture your heart

In the end, it was my heart stomped, torn, and ripped apart

Some days I felt legit; some days I wanted to quit

So naïve to believe our differences could maintain a relationship

Ferocious arguments would lead to a cold make-up

Making it effortless to design and compose the break up

Senryu Intermission

As I look in her artful eyes,
I question the truth
behind her lies.

I've been told not to go into relationships with expectations. That's impossible when women over hype themselves. The ways they've described themselves to me made me think I was getting a Rolls-Royce. I didn't anticipate ending up with a used Honda Civic.

Love Turned To Lust

Love

intense, blind

cherishing, infatuating, delighting

crush, affection, misery, apathy

affecting, agonizing, distressing

bitter, painful

Lust

Love

amity, adulation

yearning, enchanting, enthralling

friendship, allegiance, hate, berate,

neglecting, disrespecting, loathing

vile, immoral

Lust

Love

taste, fondness

tempting, alluring, enticing

attention, affection, disgrace, degrade

disparaging, deteriorating, diminishing

dreadful, atrocious

Lust

Cinquain
Loving
an adjective
falsely used by women
who are spiteful, immature, and
selfish

Somehow

You took me so high, and

Somehow

You made me feel loved, but

Somehow

I had to fight for your time, then

Somehow

My love turned to lust, then

Somehow

I was uncomfortable, and

Somehow

Your sex was undesirable, but

Somehow

Everything was wonderful, then

Somehow

Our differences were reconcilable, then

Somehow

Your deceitful hugs made me smile, and

Somehow

I endured your cattiness, but

Somehow

Your kisses were achingly vile, then

Somehow

Disgust overtook my happiness, then

Somehow

Your words grabbed my attention, and

Somehow

All still wasn't forgiven, but

Somehow

I fell into your trap again, then

Somehow

I wanted you back again

James R. Dixon

Senryu Intermission

The mind of a woman
from my perspective
is manipulation.

I find it funny, yet disturbing when women preach the same soliloquy. Based on my experiences, they preach 50/50 love, yet they only give a thirty percent effort. But rather than blame them, I have no choice but to blame myself. She asked for my car, asked to utilize my income to keep a roof over her head, and then to cosign for her student loans. It was shameful on my behalf for even considering those unjust statutes just to keep her in my life. I was too blinded to see her selfish mentality. While her ex-boyfriend was in prison, I was making up the bed he used to sleep in. I was cleaning up his mistakes while she plotted her ulterior motives and never took responsibility for any of the corrupt things she did.

Incompatible

**I deem you incompatible
Unable to exist with me in harmony!**

Spoiled by your presence
My feelings became my convictions
I had to make you distant
To compensate for the pain in my heart you've inflicted

The essence of you was shy to speak when around me
Never mind your personality
Your elegance was the cause of my irritation
Your beauty made it painful for me to see you
Like a statuesque figure I could only stare at
But not speak to
The fact it's easy for you to have a dark heart
Leaves my impression of you in disgust
When momentarily I've longed for your love
Now I don't even lust

I deem you incompatible!

No Response…

After I wrote a poem to you confessing my love
Upon waking up in your bed

No Response…

After I wrote a song for you confessing my love
Rather than read it, I sang it to you instead

James R. Dixon

I deem you incompatible,
Unable to hear my heart cry!

Bored to death by your words
Our conversations made me feel like
I was your preacher
Desperate for you to expedite your emotional outpour
I wish your personality
Was as voluptuous as your physical features
32-C's should allow me to see right through you
As I lay my head to rest
I lay motion-less in a sea of you
The thickness your thighs provide
Should ignite an invitation
Through the advancement of your eyes
The soft touch of your glossed lips
Arouses my blood and
Conjugates every aspect of my attention
Along with your sensual form
And the impact your walk has on your hips
If only your personality could be that thick

I deem you incompatible!

Behind Wounded Eyes

The power of a kiss to wounded eyes
Can feel like bliss in amid, misty skies
Can make you shiver, quiver, shake, and fly
Can make you feel so jovial inside
But the power of her kiss made me cry
Questioning all the truths behind her lies
Her cute smile devious and bonafide
Made me feel weak, frail, and fragile inside

The power of a touch to wounded hands
Can convey feelings you don't understand
Can arouse desires hard to withstand
Can provoke emotions you can expand
But the power of her touch made me bland
My irregular heart crushed by her hands
My alluring dreams she misunderstands
Made me feel foul and our bond could disband

Quinzaine
Love might equate to prison
Why do I feel trapped?
Am I trapped?

My Picture, Your Picture

My picture says a thousand words
A story that was never heard
Ticklish eyes; vision slightly blurred
Graceful eyebrows looking incurred
Charmed smile and love isn't conserved
Gentle lips speaking words misheard
Stern posture with love undeterred
My picture speaks words overheard

Your picture says a thousand words
A story that was often heard
Knavish eyes with feelings reserved
Painted eyebrows looking petered
Forged smile with emotions deferred
Vile lips speaking foul words uncured
Hunched posture; awareness demurred
Your picture is grim and absurd

Cinquain
Pictures
often times say
a thousand words and yours
signifies each synonym of
evil

Senryu Intermission

I opened up doors for you.
You walked through them
showing no gratitude.

Looks can be deceiving! But the description in "Your Picture" was accurate. I stimulated her with meaningful conversation. Mentally, she wasn't thinking "I can potentially build a future with this man." Taking my kindness for weakness was an understatement as she secretly architected my demise. I deem her incompatible!

Ode To Nice Guys

This is an ode to nice guys
Who finish last as a result of
Encountering fictitious women
Who sells us dreams and fantasies
Forcing us to think they want
A good man, marriage, and family
But their lack of effort and attentiveness
Breaks the hearts of us nice guys as we
Self consciously ponder the reasons a
Long-term relationship wasn't of common interest

This is an ode to nice guys
Who finish last as a result of
Encountering scandalous women
Who manipulate us for their personal gain
They impose their will on us
By batting their eyelids
Giving an aloof hug with an occasional kiss
Placing our hands on their breasts
As we express our displeasures, we're encouraged to be quiet
As they offer us sex in return for our silence

Everything

I love EVERYTHING about you!

Just loosen up your pants
Untuck your shirt
So everyone won't look at you
Weird from a distance

But, simultaneously
I love EVERYTHING about you!

Just be more aggressive
Man handle me in public
Dominate our conversations
As others will find it to be impressive

Nevertheless
I love EVERYTHING about you!

Just don't be so wordy
Limit your vocabulary
Speak with a speech impediment
So you don't come across as nerdy

James R. Dixon

Other than that
I love EVERYTHING about you!

Just be more aware of my needs
Accomplish your goals and dreams
To support and take care of me
Make me your one and only priority

To sum it all up
I love EVERYTHING about you!

Just change your appearance
Modify your personality
Concede to your coherence
Disregard your feelings and be more adherent

Senryu Intermission

I love everything
about you except
this, that, and
some other things.

For me to succumb to the pressure of believing nothing I do is ever good enough is comical. There's a fine line between accepting someone for who they are and accepting someone for who they can be. But, manipulating someone into being who you want them to be is selfish. It almost seems as if it gives the women I've encountered instant gratification by changing me into who they want me to be. They constantly question my mannerisms as if they don't appreciate them. That is until they encounter the "bad boy" they so eloquently lust over who verbally and physically abuse them, impregnates them, and then leaves them to fend for themselves.

Disclaimer

I met a good woman; at least I was convinced
Apparently, I failed to read the fine print

"I want a man who is six feet tall plus an inch
Preferably with a jail or prison stint
A man who communicates with a speech impediment
A man who sends me gifts with serial barcode imprints

A selfish, careless bad boy with no respect
A pompous jerk with minimal intellect
A man with multiple children he neglects
One whose reputation I have to protect

I want a man who's a woman abuser
One who's a minuscule-minded loser
A lazy, passive, apathetic moocher
An alcoholic dope head with no future

A man who would sell me out for a free meal
One who would strike me then tell me my wounds will heal
One who couldn't care less about how I feel
A vile, deceptive man who lies, cheats, and steals"

I wish I knew all of this before I claimed her
Next time I'll be sure to read the disclaimer

Quinzaine
The fine print reveals her flaws
How did she hide them?
Are there more?

88

The Clean Up Man

Troubled, scorned woman has to explain to her daughter

The heist committed by her baby's father after

Experiencing the bad boy she's placed on a pedestal

Come to find out he's a cynical asshole; now she's

> **Asking me questions like:**
> *Did you think about me much after we broke up?*
> *Where did we go wrong?*
> *Why couldn't we reconcile?*
> *Do you remember you loved me so much you wrote me letters, poems, and songs?*

She's seemingly realized the grass wasn't greener on the other side

All of a sudden, I don't seem so bad anymore

Now that she's locked in the solitary confines
of her bad decisions

Her restitution lies in goading me into being the father
of her abandoned children

Looking for me to wean her off the intoxicated bottle
of her bad boy's deity

Reintroduce her to my gentlemen's 12 step program
and reintegrate her back into society

James R. Dixon

Her baby's father leaves them home with limited
diapers, food, and comfort

Extorting money to fulfill his end of the child support

Now each passing day she calls me twice

> **Asking me questions like:**
> *Do you think we'll work out now?*
> *Can we start all over?*
> *Will you give me another chance?*
> *Can the love, attention, and affection you once had for me be conjured up again?*

All the poems I wrote about her started to resonate

From the *First* and *Second Date*

To *Those Three Words* and the *Honeymoon Phase*

All of a sudden, she didn't think I was *Too Much*

All of a sudden our *Breakdowns in Communication*
can be justified with my touch

All of a sudden she's willing to embrace everything *I've Longed* for

Now she's nagging me with questions about what I want out of life

Uttering words like love, attention, affection, husband,
provider, and protector

Preaching the same soliloquy "I want to be part of your life"

While continuously

Asking me questions like:
Don't you believe we'd make a great team?
Don't you envision yourself having a family?
Wouldn't sex with me be a consummated dream?
Don't you think you would enjoy my company?

Hell bent on making me the guardian of her fatherless children

Anticipating me to bail her out of her self-inflicted prison

Never will her words hold weight in my opinion

Never will her words be taken into consideration

James R. Dixon

Senryu Intermission

One divorce with an
annulment pending,
two baby fathers, three kids.

Once a victim of a broken home, she vowed not to reenact that lifestyle. Prior to her broken home she struggles to rebuild, I attempted to pursue her. Apparently, the gentleman routine was played out because she let the "bad boys" run rampant throughout her house. Upon the realization of her bad boy's short life span, she was willing to embrace a gentleman. Little does she know, her trials and tribulations have no bearing on me.

Slip Away

How could I be so blind

Back in the day

To ignore her

Advances and let her slip away

I made a mistake

I regretfully have to pay

Let me explain

What I'm trying to say

It all started as a

Kindergarten crush in high school

She had on me

When I was twice the fool

I didn't understand

Her feelings were true

I let her slip away

Now what was I to do

James R. Dixon

She showed deep concern

With me being with other women

Knowing they would

Treat me bad and she didn't

Want to see me go down that route

So she would be

That protective superwoman

Who would be there for me

It was no secret

She really cared for me

She would sing songs to me

And write poems constantly

Writing me love letters

Every here and there

In hope that in the late night

I would stroke her hair

Now my integrity was in question

I made such a big fuss

About her skin complexion

That I failed to realize

Her personality stimulated me to the point

She gave me a mental erection

Slip Away

Just when I never thought

I would see her again

We reconnected in college

But some things never change

I didn't grow out of my high school ways

I acted the same

Quickly realizing she wasn't attracted

To me playing games

Completely understood

So the first thing I said was "I missed you"

It would've been worse

Had I attempted to kiss her

Upon placement of the valiant offer

I dissed her

Now still till this day

It's hard for me to resist her

James R. Dixon

Who knew the time she spent with me

Made her friends jealous

I didn't ask her to be exclusive

Due to me being cocky and overzealous

Now I realize the mistakes I've made

Were in other women I've dated

If I was with her, four years of my life

Wouldn't have been wasted

From every hug she gave me

Her touch was so warm

I felt complacent

Being held in her arms

I just wanted to be with her

Forget trying to score

I was dedicated to giving her

Everything she's longed for

Now my integrity was in question

I made such a big fuss

About her skin complexion

That I failed to realize

Her personality stimulated me to the point

She gave me a mental erection

Slip Away

I truly understand

That it's too late now

She's a taken woman

And I'll never question how

She's very beautiful

She's goal oriented, comical, and smart

I hope whoever receives her

Takes care of her heart

But I'm sorry

I can't help but to think again

About a future with us

And where we could've been

Where do I begin

To tell her where my broken heart began

It killed me to see her

The last three years with him

James R. Dixon

I had multiple chances

To ask her to become exclusive

Stupid me for thinking

I had all the time in the world

I was under the impression

She only had eyes for me

As mentioned, I let her slip away

As I was too blind to see

She has a life of her own

That didn't revolve around me

I just wish I had

One more opportunity

To see her; to tell her I still love her

And I wish her all the best

As far as other women go

She's truly above all the rest

Now my integrity was in question

I made such a big fuss

About her skin complexion

That I failed to realize

Her personality stimulated me to the point

She gave me a mental erection

Senryu Intermission

Not pursuing her
when I had the chance
is a mistake I'll regret.

They say "you never know what you have until it's gone." Truth is, I never had her to begin with. So what was I truly missing? I missed a phenomenal woman who commands my undivided attention. I missed a woman whose personality served as the center of my weakness. I missed a woman whose essence had me spinning in a whole other direction. I missed a woman who expected me to show her my true feelings.

Relationship Revelation

Reality quickly set in as my

Expectations about women grew with their verbiage

Leading me to dismiss my integrity and adhere to their trustworthiness

Allowing sweet nothings and a kiss to taint my better judgment

Trembling at every woman's slightest bit of discomfort

I would emasculate myself so they wouldn't suffer

Overlooking my nourishment to put food on their table

Needless to say, I put them first because I loved them

Spending hundreds of dollars on miscellaneous things

Helping pay their bills, tuition, and grocery shopping

I was only interested in being their comforter

Putting my wants, needs, and feelings on the back burner

Reality quickly set in as my

Evaluation of myself in relationships taught me

Valuable lessons about financial and sexual abstinence

Elevating myself should be at the forefront of my mind

Leaving all minuscule things and corrupt people behind

At last, in conjunction with God, I am at peace again

Turning all negatives and unfinished business into positives and completion

In the future, I will handle relationships with a higher degree of diplomacy

Optimistic about finding love and attention; not just affection

No longer putting myself at the mercy of women

Dear Future Wife

Dear Future Wife,

We may or may not have met yet,
but I hope our marriage will be great.
I hope we will build a foundation so strong
that not even our pride, ego, and stubbornness
will cause it to break.
I hope we accrue years of memories
we will never forget.
We can one day sit on the couch
reviewing albums full of recycled photos
so we can laugh and cry as we
commemorate the day we first met.

Dear Future Wife,

I don't want perfection
I'd rather have you instead!
My promise: I'll always cherish our relationship.
I'll never make the same mistakes my father did.
I won't attempt a marriage with you after several divorces
and putting my children in precarious situations.
I won't overstep your authority creating a dictatorship.
I won't subject you to gender discrimination.
I won't leave you alone
to babysit, cook, and clean every dish
while I'm out gambling;
essentially leaving you my ass to kiss.

Dear Future Wife,

I will treat you like royalty!
No, really, royalty!
Most superficial women view royalty as
luxury cars, five star living,
material things, and fine dining.
But not you! You're different!
You consider the little things to be more important.
Like waking up to a home cooked
breakfast in the morning.
Cuddling on the couch watching reality television
doesn't sound so boring.
Everything from texting each other around the clock,
to grocery shopping, to getting our tires rotated,
to jogging around the block
are methods worth employing.
Regardless of what we do
the time I spend with you
is what I'll mostly be enjoying.

Dear Future Wife,

I don't want perfection
I'd rather have you instead!
My promise: I'll give you everything you need.
I'll give you consistent love, attention, and affection.
I'll be a husband; a provider of support and protection.
Every year as we celebrate our anniversary
I'll anticipate these words to say
"I love you just as much if not more
than I did on our wedding day."

Sincerely,
Your Future Husband!

Acknowledgments

I want to give a huge thank you to everyone who took time out of their busy schedules to rejoin me by reading my third book. This being my third book, I wanted to provide a great story about my personal relationship trials and tribulations, fond moments, and the valuable lessons I've learned.

I enjoy writing non-fiction material which is why I continue to use my past experiences in life as my muse. I hope many of you can relate to a few poems in this book. Maybe you have experienced a few situations similar to ones that I've been through and have described in Love, Attention, and Affection.

I want to give a special "thank you" to those who've supported "The Other Me (My Moment of Honesty)" and "Broken Silence"! For those who haven't gotten a chance to read my first and second books, it's not too late.

James R. Dixon

For more information on
"Love, Attention, and Affection,"
upcoming projects, questions or
feedback, feel free to contact
me via social media:

Facebook: James R. Dixon
Instagram: JRDIXON87

James R. Dixon is the author of three non-fiction poetry books. He has obtained his Bachelor's degree in Technical Management with a concentration in Hospitality Management from DeVry University. He has also obtained his Master's degree in Human Resources Management from Keller Graduate School of Management. He spends his days working as a full time independently published author.

James R. Dixon

Previous Release

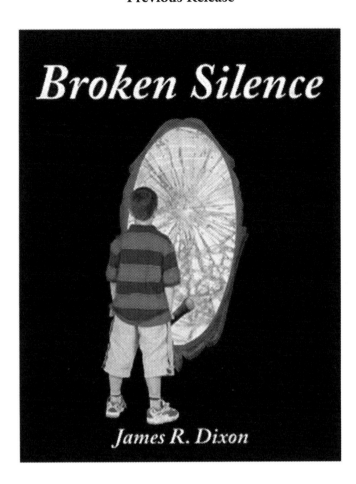

Broken Silence presents a collection of very personal poems that get to the heart of who author James R. Dixon is and what he has to say. He believes that sometimes the quiet ones have the most to say, but getting others to hear them can be a problem. Being different can mean that you may find yourself explaining your actions to others. Dixon has written Broken Silence to explain his feelings and emotions on many subjects that are important to him, as well as to change everyone's preconceived notions about him.

After years of being persecuted by others who don't approve of him, Broken Silence is also his breakthrough collection explaining his thoughts and feelings on relationships and other personal issues. Divided into four sections covering love, emotions, resilience, and good, these poems seek to offer hope and inspiration to others who are struggling to find themselves in the world.

Previous Release

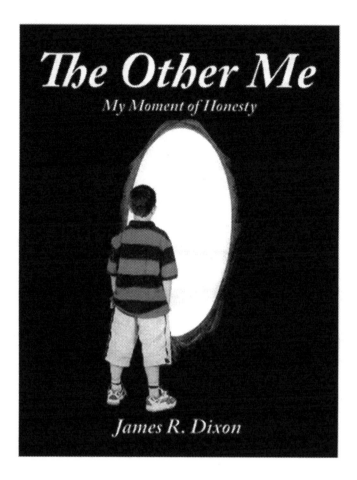

The Other Me presents a collection of very personal poems by author James R. Dixon. It is based on misconceptions placed on an individual's personality. He feels as though many people have been perceived a certain way by others and for the most part, those preconceived notions are wrong. With that said, that puts people in the position to have to defend themselves against those who misjudge them. "The Other Me" is his self-defense. The poems in the book are broken into four sections that determine the makeup of him and his personality.

James R. Dixon likes to say "the quiet ones have the most to say, but the problem is getting others to hear them." So at the conclusion of this book, maybe a few people will finally hear him.

Printed in the United States
By Bookmasters